MACMILLAN
PRE-INTERMEDIATE

AMBROSE BIERCE

Owl Creek Bridge
and Other Stories

Retold by Stephen Colbourn

MACMILLAN

MACMILLAN READERS
PRE-INTERMEDIATE LEVEL

Founding Editor: John Milne

The Macmillan Readers provide a choice of enjoyable reading materials for learners of English. The series is published at six levels—Starter, Beginner, Elementary, Pre-intermediate, Intermediate and Upper.

Level Control
Information, structure and vocabulary are controlled to suit the students' ability at each level.

The number of words at each level:

Starter	about 300 basic words
Beginner	about 600 basic words
Elementary	about 1100 basic words
Pre-intermediate	about 1400 basic words
Intermediate	about 1600 basic words
Upper	about 2200 basic words

Vocabulary
Some difficult words and phrases in this book are important for understanding the story. Some of these words are explained in the story, some are shown in the pictures, and others are marked with a number like this: ...³. Words with a number are explained in the *Glossary* at the end of the book.

Answer Keys
Answer Keys for the *Points for Understanding* and the *Exercises* section can be found at www.macmillanenglish.com.

Contents

A Note About These Stories	4
The American Civil War	4
The Places in These Stories	7
A Note About the Author	8
A Picture Dictionary	9
OWL CREEK BRIDGE	11
BEYOND THE WALL	18
AN ADVENTURE AT BROWNVILLE	28
THE DAMNED THING	39
ONE OF THE MISSING	47
THE STRANGER	54
THREE AND ONE ARE ONE	60
KILLED AT RESACA	65
Points for Understanding	72
Glossary	74
Exercises	80

A Note About These Stories

The American Civil War
America declared independence[1] from Great Britain in 1776, and after this, the republic grew very quickly. People came from many countries to start a new life in America. They divided the land into areas called states and territories. As more and more people came to America, they traveled west. They moved onto land that was the home of many different groups of Native Americans, and made their own homes there. In the eighteenth century, most of the states were in the north and east of the country. The territories, larger areas of land, were in the west. As time passed, more territories in the west were divided and became new states.

Great numbers of Africans were taken from their own countries and brought to America. African men, women and children were bought by rich farmers and became slaves. They worked in the fields and they were servants in the landowners' houses. The slaves could not leave the farms. They belonged to the landowners. Slaves could not own property and they were not paid for their work. The owners of the largest farms—plantations—became rich because of slavery.

Most of America's crops of food, cotton and tobacco grew on plantations in the southern states. America's main centers of manufacturing, industry, finance and government were in cities in the northern states. Soon more centers of industry and manufacturing developed in the middle and west of the country. The people of the south became angry because the northern, mid-western and eastern states had more power and more wealth.

In 1860, there were about thirty-one million people living in a union of thirty-four states. By this time, most people in the northern states did not own slaves. And soon many northerners began to speak against slavery.

On March 4th, 1861, Abraham Lincoln became President of the United States. He did not want people in the new western territories to own slaves. And his supporters[2] agreed with him.

Southerners disagreed with laws that were made in Washington, the capital in the north. They wanted to have their own government and they wanted to be independent. They also wanted to own slaves. Eleven states in the south left the Union. They became the Confederate States of America. The capital city of the Confederacy was Richmond, in Virginia. America was now divided into two groups, Unionists and Confederates. Each group had their own government and army.

On April 12th, 1861, Confederate soldiers fired their guns at Union soldiers in Fort Sumter[3]. President Abraham Lincoln immediately asked men to join the Union Army. He asked them to defend[4] their land against the invaders[5] from the south. A war began between the Confederates and the Unionists. Americans fought Americans. They were fighting a civil war.

At the start of the war, the Confederates won the battles because they had the best commanding officers[6]. But the Unionists had more soldiers, equipment and weapons. They placed their ships across the rivers and seaports in the south, so that the Confederates could not get food, equipment and weapons from overseas. On July 1st, 1863, a long battle was fought in Gettysburg, Pennsylvania. The fighting continued for two days, and the Confederates were defeated[7]. Twenty-eight thousand Confederate soldiers died. The Unionists won the Battle of Gettysburg, but twenty-three thousand of their soldiers died.

As General Sherman marched his Union Army through the southern states of Tennessee and Georgia, he destroyed[8] farms and crops. The men of the south became weak and hungry and could not fight. On April 9th, 1865, General Lee, the commander of the Confederate Army surrendered[9]. More than six hundred thousand men had died in the Civil War, and more than one million men were injured. On April 14th, President Lincoln was murdered while he watched a play in a theater. Soon after Lincoln's death, slavery was abolished[10] in the U.S.

The civil war in America was the first "modern" war. It was the first time that soldiers were taken to battles on trains, and in iron ships. Trains could carry many thousands of men long distances on railroads[11]. Soldiers were able to fight more strongly if they did not have to walk too many miles to the battles. Commanders of armies sent messages very quickly using telegraph machines[12]. It was also the first time people could see photographs of a war in their newspapers.

The Places in These Stories

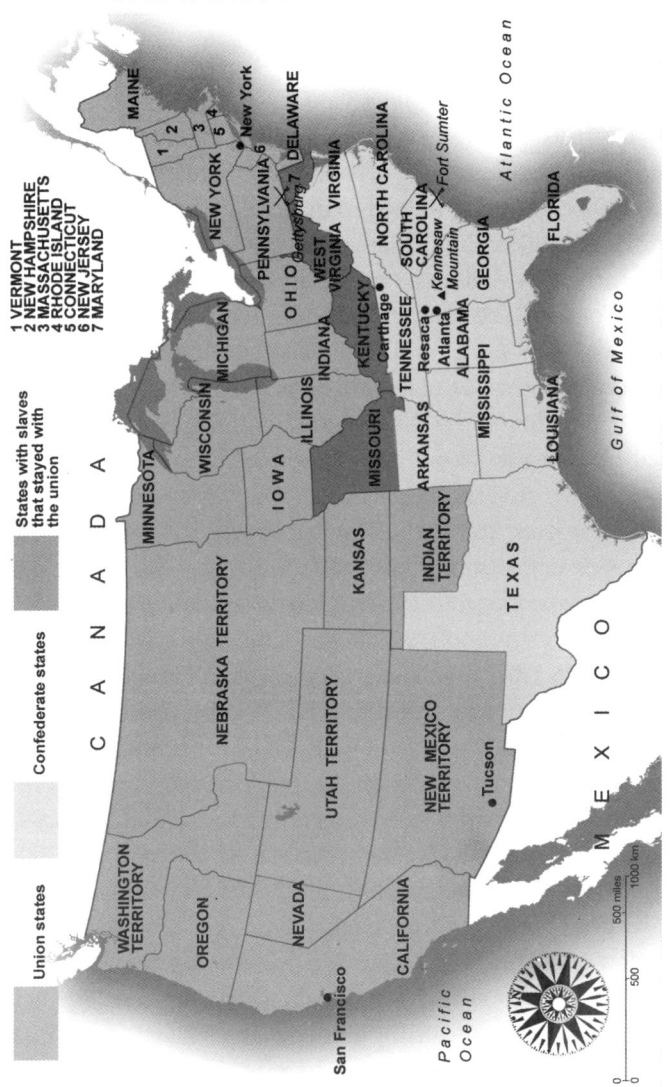

America during the Civil War 1861–1865

A Note About the Author

Ambrose Gwinnett Bierce was an American journalist and writer. He was born in Meigs County, in the state of Ohio, on June 24th, 1842, but he grew up in the state of Indiana. When the American Civil War began, Bierce became an officer in the Union Army. He helped to make maps for the Unionists.

Bierce worked in Britain between 1872 and 1876. Then he returned to America, and went to San Francisco on the West Coast. He became the editor of the newspapers, the *San Francisco News-Letter* and the *California Advertiser*. He wrote reports about theater plays and books.

Bierce admired the American writer, Edgar Allan Poe. He liked Poe's stories about ghosts, horror and mystery. Many of Bierce's own stories were about strange mysteries and ghosts. But his stories about the American Civil War made him famous. A collection of Bierce's stories was published in *Tales of Soldiers and Civilians* (1891). His most famous story, which is the first in this book, is *An Occurrence at Owl Creek Bridge*.

Between 1887 and 1906, Bierce collected amusing words and speeches that he heard or read. A book containing these words and sayings was published in 1906. It was called *The Cynic's Word Book*. The book was published for a second time in 1911, and the title was changed to *The Devil's Dictionary*.

From 1909 to 1912, *The Collected Works* were published. These twelve books contained all of Bierce's writings.

In 1913, when he was seventy-one, Ambrose Bierce went to Mexico. There was a war in Mexico at this time, and Bierce wrote newspaper reports about the fighting. Ambrose Bierce disappeared during a battle at Ojinaga, on January 11th, 1914. His body was never found.

A Picture Dictionary

- Apache
- bear
- tower
- second storey
- first storey
- mountain lion
- deer
- straw hat
- brim
- shotgun
- quail
- cab

OWL CREEK BRIDGE

A man stood on the edge of a railroad bridge in Alabama. His feet were on one end of a plank. Standing on the other end of this long flat piece of wood were two soldiers. An officer stood a few yards away from the soldiers and watched what was happening.

The man looked down at the Owl Creek River that flowed twenty feet below him. One end of a long rope was tied to the railroad bridge. The other end of the rope was tied around the man's neck. His hands were tied behind his back with a short cord.

The man turned and looked around him. A railroad track came out of a forest and ran across the wooden bridge to a small fort. The fort stood on the northern bank of the river. Soldiers with rifles guarded[13] each end of the bridge.

All the soldiers wore blue uniforms. They were soldiers of the Union Army and they were a long way from their homes in the north.

The man with the rope around his neck was not far from his home. His name was Peyton Farquhar. Peyton's home and his family were on the other side of the forest. But Peyton was not going to see them again. He was going to be hanged. When the two soldiers stepped off the plank, one end of it would lift up and Peyton would fall. When he fell, the rope would break his neck.

It was sunrise on a summer day. The sun was coming up above the trees in the east. Peyton looked down at the river below him again. The water was deep. Could he break the

Peyton looked down at the river below him.

Owl Creek Bridge

cord and free his hands? Could he jump into the river, swim away, and escape?

Peyton was not a soldier, he was a rich landowner. He was thirty-five years old and he wore fine clothes. He was a well educated gentleman. He had a handsome face, long hair and a dark beard and mustache. Members of Peyton's family had lived in the southern state of Alabama for a hundred years. Slaves worked on his plantation. Now the Union Army—the Yankees—had invaded the Confederate state of Alabama. Peyton was not a soldier in the Confederate Army. But he wanted to defend his home against the invaders from the north.

A man had visited Peyton's house two days earlier and he had given Peyton an idea. The man had been wearing a gray uniform. He had told Peyton that he was a Confederate scout. The scout watched where and when Yankee regiments moved and how many men there were. Then he reported this information to his commanding officer.

"We tried to stop the Yankees moving further into this state. We destroyed the railroad track," the scout told Peyton. "But they repaired the track. A group of Yankees have now reached the bridge over Owl Creek. There are only a few hundred Yankee soldiers at the creek now, but soon there will be many more. They'll come on trains."

"How can we stop them?" asked Peyton.

"We need more of our own men," said the soldier. "More of our soldiers *are* coming. We can keep the Yankees at the river, but we need to delay them. We must keep them on the northern side of the bridge. Our men are not far away."

"I know Owl Creek Bridge," said Peyton. "In winter, the rain carries tree branches down the river. Branches are

Owl Creek Bridge

trapped under the bridge now. I'll make a fire in the branches. They'll burn easily and so will the wooden bridge. I'll burn the bridge!"

"Be careful," said the scout. "If the Yankees catch you, they'll hang you."

So Peyton had gone to Owl Creek Bridge before sunrise. He had moved quietly along the southern bank of the river, but the bridge was well-guarded. Union soldiers had caught Peyton before he burned the bridge. And now he stood on the edge of the bridge with a rope around his neck.

Peyton looked down at a piece of wood that floated[14] on the surface of the water. The river was deep and the water was moving very fast. He looked up at the sky. The bright sun had now risen above the trees. The short rope that was tied around Peyton's hands was too strong. He could not break the cord and he could not untie it. Peyton closed his eyes and thought about his wife and children. He did not want to die.

The Yankee officer shouted an order. The soldiers stepped off the wooden plank and Peyton fell toward the river. He felt a sharp pain in his neck. Then he heard a loud noise—SNAP! The rope had broken! Peyton fell into the river and went down and down into the deep dark water.

As soon as the ropes were wet, they became loose. The cord around Peyton's hands was no longer tight. He pulled the cord from his hands, and the rope around his neck fell away. Peyton was a strong swimmer. Now his hands were free and he could swim up through the water. He kicked his legs and went up toward the surface.

Peyton opened his eyes and saw daylight. He was glad to be alive. He breathed deeply. He looked at the sky and the trees as if he was seeing them for the first time. The colors of

Owl Creek Bridge

the sky and the leaves on the trees were bright and strong.

Suddenly he heard loud voices. The soldiers were shouting as they looked down from the bridge. They were aiming their rifles down at the water.

Peyton heard the sound of a gun firing. Then he heard a bullet splash into the water and he saw a small cloud of smoke on the bridge. All the soldiers on the bridge were looking at him. They were aiming their rifles at him. One of the soldiers had fired his gun at Peyton. Peyton dove under the surface of the water and began to swim away from the bridge.

All the soldiers fired their rifles. It took them half a minute to reload[15] their guns. But Peyton was not far enough away from the bridge. The soldiers could still shoot him before he reached a safer place! Peyton swam faster.

Suddenly he heard a loud whistling sound. The guards had fired the cannon[16] that was in the small fort at the northern end of the bridge. There was a terrible noise as the cannon shell exploded. BOOM! Pieces of the shell crashed into the trees on the bank of the river. The cannon fired again. Another shell crashed in the river near Peyton's head. He began to swim quickly toward the southern bank of the river. The soldiers on the bridge fired their rifles again.

Peyton reached the river bank. The water was shallow here. His feet touched the soft sand at the bottom of the river and he stood up. He ran out of the water, toward the trees. As he ran, he held his head low. At any moment, a bullet might hit his back. Peyton ran into the forest and hid behind a large tree for a few minutes. Was he safe?

The Yankee soldiers could not see Peyton now, but he knew that he must go further into the forest. The cannon

Owl Creek Bridge

fired again and another shell crashed through the trees. The soldiers shouted as they ran across the bridge and came into the trees. Peyton ran deeper into the forest.

A strange light shone through the trees. Peyton felt as if he was in a dream. The leaves of the trees shone like bright green jewels. The smell of the flowers was strong and sweet.

It was warm in the forest and Peyton was tired. He wanted to rest. He wanted to stay here forever. But he had to escape from the Yankees. He had to go home.

Peyton walked on and on. Was there no end to the forest? Peyton had lived near this forest all his life, but he did not recognize[17] any of it. He did not know where he was. This was a wild, strange place.

The sun rose higher in the sky. Peyton was hungry and tired, but he thought about his home and his family. He must go home—he must see his wife and children. He had to walk south, so he walked with the sun on his right side. He walked all day. He walked until the sun set and night fell.

At last he came to a path in the forest. The path was as straight as a city street. The tall trees on both sides of the path were like black walls. They went straight ahead like the lines on the plan of a building. When Peyton looked up, he saw bright stars in the dark sky. But he did not recognize them. They did not look like the stars that he remembered. He heard voices whispering in the forest. The trees were talking in a language that he did not understand.

Peyton was very hot and very tired. He was thirsty too, but he did not stop to find water. He walked along the straight path. He was not far from his home.

On and on he walked. He was half-asleep and half-awake.

Owl Creek Bridge

The danger and excitement on the bridge had made Peyton extremely tired. His neck was very painful but he walked on. He knew that his house was near. It was at the end of the path. He was almost home. He was almost safe. Here the ground was soft. He no longer felt his feet moving on the soft grass. He forgot his hunger and thirst and pain.

———

Suddenly it is daylight and Peyton is standing in front of his own home. He must have traveled all through the night. He pushes open his garden gate. His sweet wife is waiting for him on the steps of his house. She is smiling. How beautiful she is! Everything is bright and beautiful in the morning sunshine. Everything looks the same, but it is also brighter and clearer. Peyton has come home. But as he puts his arms around his wife he feels a sudden, terrible pain in his neck. A white light shines brightly. Then there is darkness and silence.

———

Peyton Farquhar was dead. His neck was broken. His body hung from the rope under Owl Creek Bridge.

BEYOND THE WALL

I was born in the United States, but I lived in Hong Kong for many years. My business in Asia was successful and I became rich. After twenty years, I decided to visit my home in New York. On my way from Hong Kong to New York, I stayed one week in California.

I had a friend who lived in the city of San Francisco and I wanted to see him again. His name was Mohun Dampier and he had been my friend for many years. We had written many letters to each other. But recently, I had not received any news from him.

Dampier had never had a job. His father gave him a little money, so Dampier had never worked.

Dampier was a superstitious man. He believed that luck or magic could make things happen in his life. He spent most of his time reading books—strange books. Most of the books were about occult philosophy[18]. I called them books about magic.

As soon as I arrived in San Francisco, I sent a message to Dampier's house. The message said: *I am staying in San Francisco for three days. May I visit you?*

Dampier surprised me. An hour later, he sent a servant to my hotel with a reply.

Come to my house at once, my dear friend, he wrote. *Come this evening. You'll remember the house—I'm sure. It was my father's home. I live in a tower at one end of the house. You don't have to ring the bell or knock on the door. I'll tell the servants to go to bed. And I'll leave the front door of the tower open. Come up the stairs immediately. I'll be waiting for you. Please come soon.*

I rode in a cab[19] to Dampier's house. That evening, the weather was stormy. A strong wind was blowing and cold rain was falling. I had forgotten that California is cold and wet in winter. I only remembered the sunshine, not the wind and the rain.

Dampier's house was near the Pacific Ocean. It was an ugly, two-story building that was made of bricks. There was a tower at one end. The house was surrounded by a garden of many trees and beautiful plants. But now it was winter and there were no leaves on the trees or flowers on the plants.

The driver stopped his cab near the tower. Although the front door was only five yards away, I became soaked with rain as soon as I stepped out of the cab. I ran to the door of the tower and turned the handle.

The door was unlocked and I opened it. One small lamp burned on the stairway and it did not give much light. The hall was full of shadows and I could not see clearly. I climbed the stairs slowly, touching the wall with my fingers. At the top of the stairs there was another door. I opened it and went into a room that was lit with another small lamp.

Dampier came forward, held my hand and shook it. He was wearing a long silk coat and soft leather slippers on his feet. His clothes were old-fashioned[20] and strange.

We looked at each other and I was shocked. I had not seen Dampier for many years. My friend had changed a lot! He had been a handsome man but now his hair was gray and his face was very pale. There were many lines around his eyes and mouth. Dampier looked like a thin old man, but he was not older than fifty. His large and bright eyes shone strangely in the shadowy room.

"Welcome, my friend! Please sit down," he said.

Dampier offered me some wine and a cigar and we talked a little. But I am afraid that our conversation was not very interesting. Meeting friends after many years can be difficult and it can make you sad. Maybe Dampier guessed my thoughts.

"*Non sum qualis eram*—I'm not as I was," he said.

I tried to make a joke. "Your Latin hasn't improved[21]," I replied.

My friend smiled. "Latin is a dead language and I'm a dead man," he said. Then his smile disappeared and he said, "I'll die very soon."

I did not know what to say. I smoked my cigar and drank my wine. We were both silent for several minutes. Outside, the wind had stopped blowing. I wanted to leave the house.

Suddenly I heard a strange noise. TAP. TAP. TAP. It was the sound of someone, or something, knocking. Was the sound coming from one wall of the tower? TAP. TAP. TAP. The sound was not quick or loud. It was not the sound of someone knocking loudly on a door. The soft tapping sounded like someone sending a signal—a message.

Dampier had forgotten me. He was staring at the wall. There was a strange expression[22] on his face. My friend looked excited and afraid. His eyes shone brightly.

I did not know what to do. Should I go or stay? I stood up.

"I—I see that you are very tired," I said. "I'll leave. May I visit you tomorrow?"

Dampier turned his head and looked at me.

Beyond the Wall

"Please stay," he said. "There's no problem. Nobody is there."

He walked to a small window and opened it. I had not noticed[23] the window earlier.

"Look," he said.

I walked across the room and looked out of the window.

I could see nothing except the light of a street lamp and rain falling. No one was standing outside. There was no one near the wall of the tower.

"Please don't leave me," said Dampier. "I must tell you a story. You're the only man that I can tell it to. Will you listen to my story?"

I wanted to go back to my hotel. Dampier, his house and the strange noise made me feel uncomfortable. I think that I am a sensible and intelligent man. But I felt unhappy and frightened in that old tower room. However, I did not want to upset my old friend.

"Very well," I said. "I'll stay and listen."

Dampier poured me another drink and offered me another cigar. Then he began to tell his story.

"I didn't move into this house until my father died," Dampier said. "That was ten years ago, when I was about forty years old. When my father died, I got his business, his property and his money.

"Before his death, I lived in a large apartment building[24] on Rincon Hill," said Dampier. "Maybe you know that area of San Francisco? Rincon Hill was a fashionable area fifty years ago, but now it is run-down and neglected[25]. The owner of the apartment building rented out many of its small rooms. The walls of the rooms were thin. You could almost put your hand through them.

21

Beyond the Wall

"I was lucky," Dampier went on. "The rent was cheap and I had a large room in the building. No one visited me. And no one disturbed me—I could study my books quietly. I lived happily on Rincon Hill.

"One morning, as I was leaving the apartment, I saw a young girl," Dampier continued. "It was a warm day in June. She was wearing a white dress and a straw hat[26]. There were brightly-colored flowers and ribbons around the brim of the hat. Then I saw the girl's face. It's difficult to find words to describe it. Her face was strange and beautiful. I had never seen such a beautiful face before. Without thinking, I lifted my hat and bowed[27]. She looked at me with shining brown eyes, but she didn't speak. I knew that she was pleased to see me, but she didn't smile. She went into the house and shut the door. I stood and stared at the closed door. Would I see her again? Should I speak to her? Would *she* speak to *me*?

"Maybe you think that these are the thoughts of a much younger man," said Dampier. "And maybe you're right. But these feelings were new to me. I'd never been in love before. I'd spent too many years with books and too little time with people. Now I believe that you're my only friend. Soon, none of this will matter. I don't feel foolish when I talk to you."

Dampier stopped speaking for a few moments, then he went on with his story.

"The next day, I waited in my apartment. For many hours, I stared out of the window. I watched the street, but the girl didn't come out of the building. I didn't know her name, so I couldn't ask anyone about her. That night I couldn't sleep. The next morning, I sat by the window again and waited.

"Then suddenly, she came out of the apartment building and I went out too. But when I reached the street, she had disappeared. I didn't see where she had gone, so I walked around the neighborhood[28]. At last I saw her in a narrow street. We smiled at each other. She recognized me, I'm sure of that. From that time, I often went out when the girl went out. She always wore the straw hat with the brightly-colored flowers and ribbons on its brim. I didn't follow her. I simply walked around the neighborhood, and hoped to see her again.

"At last, I went to the landlady of the apartment. 'Who is the girl with the pretty face and the straw hat?' I asked her. 'She's my niece, sir,' the landlady replied. 'She's a servant in this house. She lives here because her parents are dead. She works for me—she cooks and cleans the building. I also send her to buy our food. She lives at the top of the house. Her room is next to yours, but at the top of the other staircase.'

"Oh, my friend! I wish that I'd never heard that piece of information," Dampier said to me. "The girl's room was next to mine. She was on the other side of the thin wall. At night, I put my hand on the wall and I thought of her. Was her bed by the wall? Was she sleeping only a few inches from my hand?

"I couldn't study because of the girl," said Dampier. "My mind wasn't clear. I only thought about the girl. I couldn't study my books about the occult.

"I'd never wanted to marry," Dampier went on. "I'd never wanted a wife and children. I was only interested in learning. And I could never marry a poor, uneducated servant girl. My father would never have given his permission[29]. All my money came from my father. If he had stopped giving me money...well..."

"What happened next?" I asked.

Beyond the Wall

My friend looked at me sadly.

"I stopped waiting for her and I stopped watching her. I only studied. I spent all my time reading my books. But one hot night I couldn't sleep. Thoughts were racing around and around in my mind. I thought again and again about the beautiful girl. I wanted to be with her. She was only on the other side of the wall! I tapped on the wall. I tapped very gently three times. TAP. TAP. TAP. I tapped again. TAP. TAP. TAP. Then I felt foolish. I was behaving like a boy who is in love for the first time. I got out of my bed and began to study my books.

"I was reading a strange book," Dampier said. "It was a book of occult philosophy by Necromantius[30]. You would call it a book of magic and superstition. In his book, Necromantius describes how to be a fortune-teller[31]. Necromantius also wrote about strange and terrible things that happen three times. When these things happened three times, death would come. Necromantius called this a 'fatal triad'. I believe that a fatal triad has happened to me."

"Why?" I asked. "What happened?"

"While I was alone, reading that strange book by Necromantius," said Dampier, "I heard a sound. It was a soft tapping sound. It came from beyond the wall. It was the answer to my own signal! TAP. TAP. TAP. I knew that the pretty servant girl was sending a message to me. She wanted me to come to her. I ran to the wall and tapped my signal again. TAP. TAP. TAP. But after that, there was silence. She didn't reply to any of my other signals. I listened for many hours, but I heard nothing more.

"For many days after this, I looked for the girl," Dampier said. "But I never saw her again. I tried to forget her. Then

"I ran to the wall and tapped my signal again."

one evening, I went to bed early because I was very tired. In the middle of the night, I awoke suddenly. I had heard a soft sound. I opened my eyes and sat up. I heard a soft tapping on the wall beside the bed. In a few moments, it was repeated. TAP. TAP. TAP. I was going to reply to the signal, then I stopped. The girl hadn't replied to my last messages. I would *not* reply to *her* now!"

Dampier drank a little wine and then continued.

"I lay in the bed listening," he said. "But I didn't reply. At last, I must have slept. When I awoke, it was late and I felt tired. I needed some fresh air, so I went out of my apartment. The landlady was outside my door. 'Oh, Mr Dampier,' she said. 'Have you heard the terrible news?'

"My heart began to beat quickly. My voice shook when I answered. 'W–what news?' I asked her. 'My poor niece was sick for a week,' the landlady replied. 'Didn't you know? I've seen you watching her. Didn't you know that she was ill?'

"I was shocked," said Dampier. "I didn't know what to say. Yes. I *had* looked at the girl, but I'd never spoken to her. My mind was always full of thoughts of my books and thoughts of her. How much time had passed since I had seen the girl? A few days? A week? I couldn't remember.

" 'And how is your niece now?' I asked the landlady. 'I'm sorry, sir,' the landlady replied. 'She was very ill last night and I took care of her. The poor girl made only one request. She wanted her bed to be moved. She wanted her bed to be beside the wall—the wall next to your room. So we moved her bed. This made her feel happier, poor thing. Then she touched the wall and smiled. A few hours later, she died.' "

The expression on Dampier's face was terrible. There were tears in his eyes as he continued his story.

"When I heard this news, I nearly died too," said my friend. "I didn't know what to say. What had I done? I had sent my thoughts to the girl and she had answered. I had not called out in words. I had used occult philosophy—magic—to send her a message."

Dampier was silent for a few minutes. Then he went on.

"A few days later, I heard of my father's death," said Dampier sadly. "I left the apartment on Rincon Hill and came to his house—this house. It's been my home since then. I've been waiting here, in this tower, for ten years. I've been waiting for a visitor. I wasn't expecting to see you, but your visit wasn't a surprise. Necromantius tells us how signs are repeated three times. You've heard my story. You must decide if my story has happened because of a fatal triad. I heard the tapping twice before. The first time, I tried to find the person who made the noise. The second time, many signals were sent to me but I didn't reply. Now you've heard the tapping too. That was the third time. The fatal triad is complete."

I stood up and shook Dampier's hand. My friend knew that I understood his sadness and pain. He pressed my hand with his fingers and smiled. I said goodnight. There was nothing more to say.

―――

The next morning, a servant came from Dampier's house. He brought a sad message for me. My friend, Mohun Dampier, had died in the night.

AN ADVENTURE AT BROWNVILLE

There was only one school in Brownville and I was the only teacher. Brownville was a small town and had few young people, but many visitors stayed there in the summer.

Brownville has some of the finest views in the state of California. The town lies between hills that are covered in beautiful, colorful trees. In the hills, the air is fresh and clear. Many visitors came to Brownville to improve their health. They walked on the hills and breathed the good, clean air.

I saw many of these visitors because I lived in a boarding house[32]. In summer, the house was full of guests and I talked to most of them. I ate breakfast and supper in the boarding house and spent the rest of the day at the school.

The school was not far away. It was on the other side of a hill. The distance by road was about one and a half miles, but I knew a shorter way. I could walk over the top of the hill in fifteen minutes. There was a path that ran through the forest on the hill.

I came back along this forest path late one evening. It was the last day of term. Tomorrow, the students' vacations would begin. I had stayed late at the school because I had been writing reports about the students.

The sun was going down in the sky. Its golden light shone through the trees and made long dark shadows. I was tired. I sat down on an old, fallen tree and looked at the sun setting in the darkening sky. It was calm and peaceful in the forest.

Suddenly I heard voices. One was a woman's voice, and

An Adventure at Brownville

she sounded angry. The second voice belonged to a man. It was a deep and musical voice—the voice of a singer. I could not see who was speaking, but I could hear the words clearly.

"*Don't* threaten[33] me!" the man said. "You can do nothing. Don't try to change anything, or you'll both suffer[34]."

"What do you mean?" said the woman's voice angrily. It was a cultivated voice—she spoke clearly and well. "Do you mean that you'll murder us?"

The man did not reply. I wanted to get to the boarding house. It was supper time, and I was hungry. But I did not want to pass the man and woman. I looked around and saw no one. I stood up quickly and walked on.

It was almost dark now, but suddenly I saw the two people among the trees. They were standing on the path. The man was tall and slim. He seemed to be wearing black clothes. But there were too many shadows and I could not see clearly. The woman wore a pale gray dress. They did not see me.

As I watched, the woman knelt on the ground in front of the man. She held her hands together in front of her face. Was she begging[35] for the man's help? Or was she praying that he would not hurt her? I did not like this scene. There was trouble here. I stepped behind a large tree.

When I looked at the path again, the man and woman had disappeared. I walked on until I saw the light of the lamps shining from the windows of the boarding house. The scene of the man and the woman in the forest stayed in my mind. It had made me feel unhappy and uncomfortable.

―――

I saw some new guests at breakfast the next morning. A young woman sat at a table opposite mine, but she was not the woman who I had seen last night.

An Adventure at Brownville

Then a younger lady entered the dining-room. The two young women looked very similar. And they were both extremely pretty.

When the second young lady spoke, I recognized her voice immediately. I had heard it in the forest. The two ladies were sisters. I guessed that they were about eighteen and twenty years old.

I finished my coffee and left the dining-room quickly. We were the only people in the room and I did not want to listen to their private conversation. That would be rude. And I did not want them to notice me.

I did not see the tall, slim man, but I heard him. He was in the garden of the boarding house. As I had guessed, he was a singer. He was practicing his singing. He was singing "La donna é mobile"—a song from Verdi's opera[36], *Rigoletto*.

The singer had a very good, strong voice. Maybe it was too good. Why was he in a simple boarding house in Brownville and singing in this way? This was strange. Did he want the guests to admire his voice? I walked away quickly.

When I returned to the boarding house later, I saw the elder sister. She was standing in the garden with the singer. He was dressed in black clothes. His back was turned toward me, so I could not see his face.

Brownville was a small town and it had no theaters or restaurants. So when the people of Brownville finished their work, they enjoyed gossiping[37]. I enjoyed gossiping too. Who were these unusual visitors, and what was their story?

The singer was talking easily to the younger woman. I guessed that they knew each other well. When I came into the garden, he stopped talking and turned around. He looked straight at my face.

An Adventure at Brownville

The man was not young. I guessed that he was about fifty years old. His face was extremely handsome. His hair was thick and black—as black as the clothes that he wore. And the clothes were very fine. They were smart, fashionable and well-made. They looked expensive. He could not have bought clothes like these in Brownville. I had seen pictures of opera houses in the fashionable cities of Europe. This man reminded me of the men in those pictures.

The man looked at me as if he knew the thoughts in my head. Did he know what I was *thinking*? The expression on his face was not angry or frightening. But I suddenly felt afraid. Why? I could not explain it. I only knew that I was afraid of this dark and handsome man. He was dangerous. I did not like him.

He put his hand on the young woman's arm and turned her away. Then they stepped inside the boarding house and disappeared. Neither of them spoke to me.

The landlady of the boarding house always liked to gossip. She always had the latest news and was happy to talk about it. So I asked her about the new guests.

"The two girls are Pauline and Eva Maynard and they've come from San Francisco," the landlady said. "Pauline is the older sister. The man's name is Richard Benning. He is their guardian[38]. He has taken care of the girls since their father died. Soon, when the girls are twenty one, they'll have their father's money. Meanwhile, Eva isn't well. Mr Benning believes that the good air of Brownville will improve her health."

"Mr Benning takes very good care of the two girls," the landlady went on. "He spends a lot of money on them, and on himself. But maybe he's spending their *father's* money."

An Adventure at Brownville

It was now my summer vacation. I did not have to go back to the school for several weeks. I walked on the hills and enjoyed the views and the fresh air. I often met Richard Benning and the two girls walking on the hills too. They seemed to be very happy together. Then I remembered the strange words that I had heard one of the sisters say. *"Do you mean that you'll murder us?"* Why had Eva Maynard said this?

For a short time, I forgot those frightening words. Then one morning, the people of Brownville were all talking about a tragedy. Something terrible had happened in their town. Pauline Maynard, the elder sister, had died. Many people came to the boarding house to say a few kind words.

I went into the sitting-room. Eva Maynard was standing beside the body of her dead sister and she was weeping. Pauline Maynard was lying in a wooden coffin[39]. Her face was extremely pale. She looked as if she were asleep. A crowd of people stood in the doorway of the sitting-room and stared at the scene.

Suddenly, Richard Benning pushed his way through the crowd and entered the room. He tried to hold Eva's hand, but she pulled it away. She stood up and cried out.

"It's you!" she shouted. "You've done this. You—you—YOU!"

"She doesn't know what she's saying," Richard Benning said in a soft voice. "She's had a terrible shock. She's upset."

Benning moved toward Eva, but she stepped away from him. He did not try to touch her hand again. Instead, he moved his hand in front of her face—slowly—once. Immediately Eva's eyes closed and she stood still. Then Benning held her hand and put his other arm around her

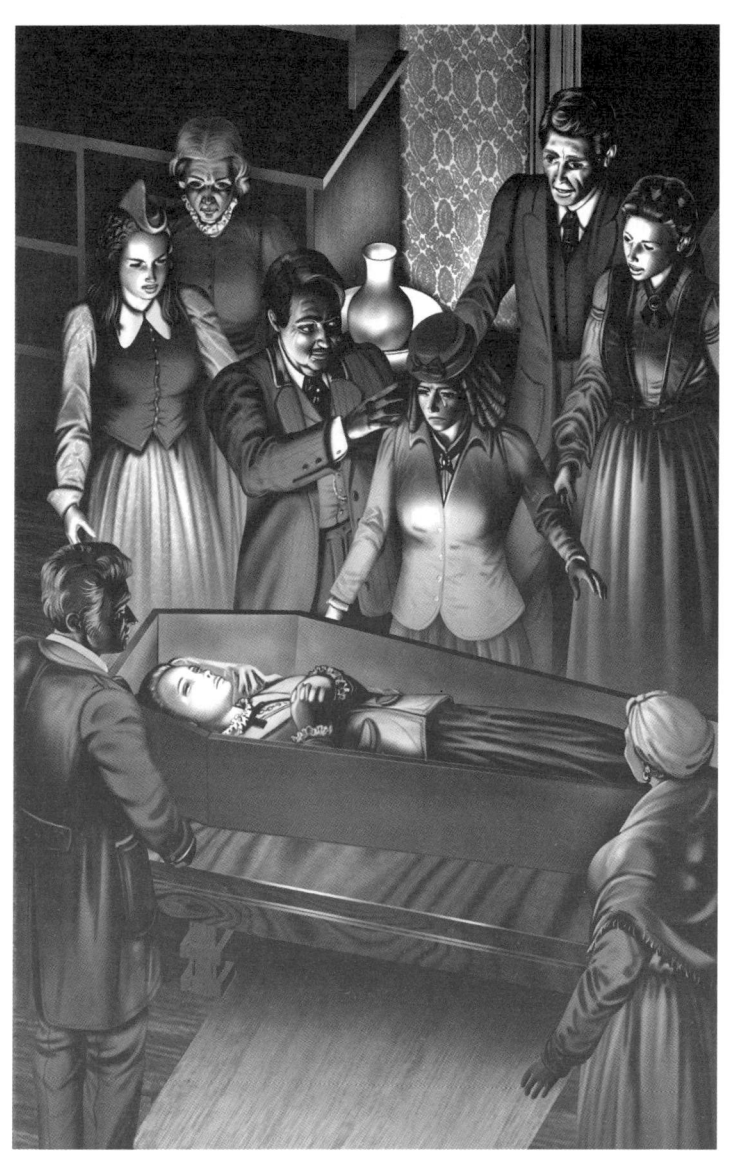

He moved his hand in front of her face—slowly—once.

An Adventure at Brownville

shoulders. Suddenly she began to weep again. Then Benning gently led the young woman out of the room.

A few days later, there was an inquest[40] in Brownville. The coroner listened to the words of Benning, a doctor, and several people in the boarding house. Then he wrote these words on Pauline's death certificate[41]: *Cause of death—heart disease.* They thought that Pauline had died suddenly because her heart was weak.

Benning sent for an undertaker[42] from San Francisco. The undertaker took Pauline's body back to the city and she was buried. Neither Benning nor Eva went to the dead girl's funeral. Many of the people of Brownville thought that this was wrong and strange.

"Poor Eva," the landlady said to me. "Her health is not good. Mr Benning is worried. He doesn't want to take her back to San Francisco. Her health might become worse if she goes to the city. It's better for her to stay here, in Brownville."

A week passed. One evening, I finished my supper and went into the garden. I saw Richard Benning and Eva Maynard standing beneath a tree. They were holding each other's hands and looking into each other's eyes. It was a very gentle and romantic scene, but it was wrong. They looked like lovers. Benning was a fifty-year-old man and Eva was not yet twenty. Also, he was her guardian. Benning should be like a father to the young woman—not a lover.

I stood in the shadows and they did not see me. I did not move, but I listened.

"You will kill me," said Eva, "I know that you killed Pauline. I beg you to kill me quickly. Let me go. Let me be at peace."

Richard Benning did not reply. He released Eva's hand

An Adventure at Brownville

and walked away. He walked up the hill to the forest where I had first seen him. As he walked, he sang. His fine voice sounded beautiful and wild. Eva stared at her guardian. As she listened, she put her hands together. She held her hands in front of her body as if she was praying.

I walked out of the shadows. Eva turned and stared at me. Maybe I had frightened her.

"Miss Maynard," I said, "I'm sorry. I came into the garden and I heard what you said. I believe that you're in danger."

"You can do nothing," she said. Her voice was soft and she had a strange expression on her face. Her eyes were large and bright. Was she ill? Or maybe she was dreaming?

I gently held Eva's hand. "You seem to be asleep," I said. "You must wake up. You said that Benning killed your sister. You said that he'll kill you too. Will you tell me about it? I'll try to help you."

"You can't help me," said Eva. "We'll be here for only a day or two more. Then we'll go away—far away. I ask you to be silent. You mustn't talk about anything that you've seen or heard here."

"But this is crazy," I said. "I'm sure that you're in danger. I must tell the police."

Eva woke up a little when she heard this. Her expression changed. She became cold and polite.

"This is my business, not yours," she said.

"But your sister died here—in Brownville," I said. "And she died suddenly. Now *you* are in danger. The people of Brownville might be in danger too. You must tell me what happened. Didn't you love your sister?"

"Yes, I loved her," said Eva. "But I love *him* more. Do you think that the police will believe you? You heard a secret

An Adventure at Brownville

conversation. If you talk about it, I'll say that your words are lies. No one will believe your story."

Suddenly she smiled. It was a beautiful, sweet smile. I could not believe her words. They were so hard and cold.

Eva held my hand tightly. "Come with me," she said. "We'll walk together. *He* will be away all night. He won't know that you've been with me. We'll walk and talk. And you'll forget what you've seen and heard. You'll forget about us."

Truly, I did not know the ways of women then. I was happy to walk in the garden with Eva Maynard. I was a little in love with this beautiful young woman. We talked about the people of Brownville. And we talked about their love of gossip. I did not want to go to my bed.

Before I said goodnight, I asked Eva to walk with me the next day.

"There's an old mill[43] on the top of the hill. Will you walk there with me tomorrow afternoon? We can enjoy the fine views from the mill."

"If *he's* not here, yes. I'll walk there with you," said Eva.

I went to bed feeling happy. I smiled happily as I fell asleep. The next morning, I awoke feeling even happier.

"Today is going to be a special day," I thought.

Eva was not in the dining-room at lunchtime. Maybe I had hoped for too much. I am only a school teacher in a small town. And I am not very rich, or very handsome. But I was not disappointed. Eva came into the garden. Benning must have gone away! I was the happiest man in the world!

Eva said nothing as I followed her up the path to the old mill. She knew the way there because she had walked to the mill many times with her guardian.

An Adventure at Brownville

Eva and I did not have a conversation, but she sang songs. She sang happy and sad songs. Her feelings changed as quickly as clouds pass across the sky. One minute—sunshine. The next minute—shadow. I was happy to be with her, whatever she felt. She walked and I followed.

When we came to the mill, she did not stop walking. She crossed an old wooden bridge and took the path up the high hill. It was the path to a place called the Eagle's Nest. This was where the path ended, on a cliff[44] high above the forest. The view from Eagle's Nest was beautiful.

I was a little afraid. The view was fine, but I did not like to go near the edge of the cliff. The ground was more than two hundred feet below us. But Eva stood on the cliff's edge and looked up, not down.

Suddenly I heard footsteps, and Richard Benning came and stood beside us.

"I saw you walking on the path," he said carelessly, "so I came up too."

Eva turned toward us. She still stood on the edge of the cliff. Her eyes were shining and she was smiling. There was a look of love on her face.

"I'm so glad that you came," she said.

She was staring at Benning. Her loving expression showed that she was telling the truth. But then I saw something else in her expression.

Eva's mouth was smiling, but suddenly there was fear in her eyes. She looked like a frightened animal. With a smile on her lips and fear in her eyes, Eva stepped backward. She fell over the edge of the cliff to the ground below.

Benning and I ran down the path to the bottom of the cliff. He got there before me.

An Adventure at Brownville

I did not want to look at Eva's body. Beautiful Eva was no longer beautiful. Benning looked at her carefully but he did not touch her.

"She's dead, quite dead," he said. "I'll go to the town and get a police officer. Please stay here with the body."

I did not know what to say. I was shocked.

Benning started to walk toward Brownville. Then he turned and looked at me.

"You saw what happened," he said carelessly. "It was an accident. Eva killed herself. I saw her step off the edge of the cliff and you saw it too."

"You're a killer!" I said. "You're a damned[45] killer! You didn't touch her, but I know that you killed her."

Benning turned his back toward me and walked away. As he walked through the forest, I heard him singing. He was singing a song from Verdi's opera, *Rigoletto*.

"La donna é mobile..."

THE DAMNED THING

It was night. Eight men were sitting together in an empty room of a small house. The only pieces of furniture were a simple wooden table and eight chairs. The only light came from a lamp on the table. One of the men was reading a book. He held the book close to the lamp, so that he could see the words on the pages.

There was a ninth man in the room. He owned the house. He was lying on the table, beneath a white sheet. The ninth man was dead.

It was quiet in the house. Outside, there were the sounds of birds and insects in the trees around the house. Visitors from the city always noticed these strange cries and calls. But the men in the room took no notice of these sounds. They heard them every day. Seven of the men were farmers and woodsmen. They worked in the fields and forests every day of the year. The skin on their faces had been burned by the sun and the wind. They were wearing hats with broad brims.

The man with the book did not look like the others. He was not wearing a broad-brimmed hat. His face was smooth, intelligent and handsome. He looked like an educated, important man. He was a coroner.

All of the men were here this evening to do an important job. An inquest was taking place in the room. The men had come to look at the dead body on the table. They had to answer this question: *How did this man die?*

The coroner was reading a diary. It belonged to the dead man. The coroner and the seven men were waiting for a

The Damned Thing

witness[46] to attend the dead man's inquest.

Suddenly, they heard the sound of a horse galloping on the road. Someone was riding quickly toward the house. The horse stopped outside, the door opened and a young man came in.

"I'm late. I'm sorry," he said.

"We've been waiting for you," said the coroner. "We must finish this job tonight. Hugh Morgan must be buried tomorrow morning. Where have you been?"

"I went to the telegraph office and sent a telegram," said the young man. "I've written a report about Hugh Morgan's death. The report will be in the San Francisco newspapers tomorrow. I'm a reporter. I write stories for the newspapers."

"You're not here to tell us a newspaper story," said the coroner. "You're here to tell us what happened to Mr Morgan. You must tell the truth. You must swear[47] that you'll do this."

"Yes. I'll tell you the truth," said the young man. "But you might not believe me."

"That isn't a good beginning," said the coroner. "Is your newspaper report different from the story that you're going to tell us?"

For a moment, the young man had an angry expression on his face. "I've come here to tell you what really happened," he said. "I promise that I'll tell you the truth. *Everything* that I say to you will be true. You can read what I wrote for the newspaper. These are the true facts. This is what I saw and heard and did. The report isn't fiction."

"Let's begin," said the coroner.

The men took off their hats. The young man lifted his right hand and began to speak slowly and clearly.

"I swear before God. I will tell the truth, the whole truth and nothing but the truth," he said.

The Damned Thing

"What is your name?" asked the coroner.
"William Harker."
"Age?"
"Twenty-seven."
"Did you know the dead man, Hugh Morgan?"
"Yes, I did."
"Were you with him when he died?"
"I was near him."

"Tell us what happened," said the coroner. "Why were you with Mr Morgan, and what did you see?"

"I was visiting him," said Harker. "Morgan and I were good friends. I live in San Francisco, but I often came here to stay with Morgan. We hunted birds and animals in the forest, and we caught fish in the rivers. Morgan and I went hunting and fishing together many times."

"Tell us what happened on the day that Mr Morgan died," said the coroner.

"We left this house at sunrise," said Harker. "We wanted to hunt quails. We took Morgan's dog with us and we both carried shotguns. Morgan told me, 'There's a field of wild oats[48] over the hill. There are many good, large quails there. They'll be good to eat.' So we went to the field. But we found something bigger than quails."

"What do you mean?" asked the coroner. "Did you find an animal?"

"Yes—er—no," said Harker. "I don't know what kind of animal it was. But I saw the oats moving in the field. Something was coming toward us. I couldn't see the animal, but I guessed that it was big. Morgan didn't say anything. He lifted his gun and aimed it at the oats."

Harker stopped speaking and looked toward the window.

The Damned Thing

"Please continue, Mr Harker," said the coroner. "What happened next?"

"I pointed at the moving plants," replied Harker. "I said, 'Morgan! If that's a deer, you won't be able to kill it with a shotgun. You'll need a more powerful gun—a rifle. But maybe it's something bigger than a deer. It might be a bear, or a mountain lion!' But Morgan didn't reply. He just aimed his gun at the oats and stared. I began to be afraid. Our shotguns wouldn't stop an angry bear or a lion."

"Mr Harker, you say that it was a big animal," said the coroner. "Do you know the difference between a bear and a lion and a deer?"

"Yes, I do, sir," said the young man quickly and angrily. "And that's the strangest part of this story. I saw the oats moving. And I heard something coming through the plants. But I couldn't see what it was. A big thing was moving toward us, but I couldn't *see* it."

"Did you speak to Mr Morgan again?" asked the coroner.

"Yes," said Harker. "I shouted, 'What is it?' But Morgan didn't reply. The animal—or thing—was coming closer and Morgan got ready to fire his gun. Suddenly he said, 'It's that Damned Thing!' He was terrified."

"Did Mr Morgan know what it was?" asked the coroner. "Is that what you believe, Mr Harker?"

"Yes, sir," Harker replied. "I believe that Morgan had seen it before. Then he fired his gun and I heard a terrible sound. It was the scream of a wild animal."

"And did you fire your gun too?" asked the coroner.

"No, I didn't. I couldn't," replied Harker. "The smoke from Morgan's gun was in my eyes. I couldn't see where to aim my own gun. Then, suddenly, Morgan dropped his gun and started to run."

*"He just aimed his gun at the oats and stared.
I began to be afraid."*

The Damned Thing

"He left you?" asked the coroner.

"Well, I *was* surprised," said Harker. "But I didn't have time to think about it. Something knocked me to the ground."

"What knocked you down?" asked the coroner.

"Well, I didn't see it. But it was soft and heavy. It moved very fast."

"And then what happened?"

"I heard wild screams near me. They were like the sounds made by dogs who are fighting. Then I saw that *Morgan* was fighting. He was on the ground. He was fighting for his life."

"Fighting *what?*" asked the coroner.

"I—I don't know," said the young man. "I couldn't see anything, or anyone. But Morgan was on the ground and there was a strange movement in the air around him. I don't know how to describe it. It seemed as if the fight was happening under water. Sometimes I couldn't see one of Morgan's hands. Sometimes his head disappeared. Then his whole body moved again."

"And did you try to help Mr Morgan?" asked the coroner.

"Of course I did. I ran toward him. But I found him like this…" Harker pointed to the dead body on the table.

"And where was the animal?" asked the coroner.

"I don't know. I only saw the oats moving again. They moved as if there was wind blowing across them. The thing—whatever it was—went into the woods. My friend was dead. I came into town to get a police officer."

"Very well," said the coroner, "we'll examine the body."

He lifted the white sheet off Morgan's body. Then he removed a handkerchief that was tied around the dead man's head. The handkerchief kept Morgan's mouth closed. The other men looked closely. One of them held the lamp high.

The Damned Thing

Its light shone on the body of the dead man.

Hugh Morgan's throat had been torn open. There were many terrible deep injuries all over his body. His clothes were soaked with blood.

"Gentlemen, you've heard Mr Harker's story," said the coroner. "You've seen Mr Morgan's body. What shall we write on the death certificate? Did a wild animal kill Mr Morgan, or was he murdered? We must decide."

The seven men went out of the room and spoke together quietly for two or three minutes.

William Harker turned toward the coroner.

"I see that you have Morgan's diary, sir," he said. "Have you read it? Does it tell us anything important?"

"I've read it quickly," said the coroner, "No, it doesn't tell us anything about the cause of Mr Morgan's death."

The seven men came back into the room. One of them stood in front of the coroner and spoke.

"We believe that Hugh Morgan was killed by a mountain lion," he said.

"Thank you, gentlemen," said the coroner. "Everyone can leave now. Mr Morgan will be buried in the morning. I'll send for an undertaker."

That was the end of the inquest. But it was not quite the end of the story.

William Harker was a writer. He wanted to read Hugh Morgan's diary and write a story about his friend's death. He stayed in the town after Morgan was buried. A few days later, Morgan's property and belongings were sold. William Harker bought the diary.

Hugh Morgan had been a lonely man who had written all his thoughts in his diary. But he had not always written days and dates in the diary. And some of the pages in the book were torn. Other pages were missing. This is what Morgan had written before his death:

My dog is behaving strangely. He barks and turns around again and again. He looks at something that isn't there. He runs after something that he can't see. This has happened several times.

2 September
Tonight, I was looking at the stars in the sky above the hill. Then something strange happened. Someone—or something—moved between me and the stars. The stars suddenly looked like a pool when you drop a stone in the water. Am I going crazy?

27 September
It's been here again. It moves around the house. Now I keep my gun beside me always. Does this Thing only come at night? Today I saw footprints in the soft ground, near the house. What's happening here? Am I going crazy?

3 October
I shall not leave my home. I will not run away because of this Thing. But it might make me crazy.

5 October
I've invited my friend, Harker, to stay here. I'll say nothing. Maybe he'll find an answer. Maybe he'll see the Thing too.

Can the dog see it? I'm sure that the dog hears it. It hears things that I can't hear. Can the dog see things that I can't see? Perhaps that is the answer. If there are sounds that men can't hear, are there colors that men can't see? Is the Damned Thing a color that men can't see?

ONE OF THE MISSING

Private Jerome Searing was a Yankee scout. He was often sent to watch the movements of enemy soldiers.

A group of army officers was standing on a hill in Georgia. They were looking south, toward a forest. They were wearing blue Yankee uniforms. A regiment of the Confederate Army was on the other side of the forest.

"Is the enemy moving forward, or retreating[49], or not moving at all?" one of the Union officers asked.

"We'll send a scout to look," replied another officer.

A few minutes later, Private Searing was sent to check the position of the Confederate regiment.

Searing was a brave man. He worked alone and he did his work well. He had sharp eyes and ears. He could see far into the distance. And he often heard sounds that other people could not hear. Now he moved silently through the forest toward the enemy regiment. In his hands, he carried a powerful rifle. Searing could shoot extremely well.

When Searing reached the edge of the forest, he stopped. He got down on his hands and knees and crawled forward slowly. He was looking for the enemy's picket line[50].

Pickets guarded the men of their regiment. They dug holes—rifle-pits—in the ground around the edge of their camp[51]. The pickets sat in the rifle-pits and aimed their guns at the enemy. Usually, there were three or four men together in each rifle-pit. The pickets took turns to sleep. While one man watched, the other men slept.

One of the Missing

Searing was looking for small mounds of earth[52] on the ground. The mounds would show Searing where the Confederates had dug their rifle-pits. The mounds would also show him where the enemy had positioned its picket line.

The scout quickly lay flat on the ground. Through a narrow opening in the bushes, he had seen a small mound of yellow earth. It was one of the enemy's rifle-pits. After a few moments, Searing slowly and carefully lifted his head. He looked at the mound of earth for several more minutes. Then he stood up and walked forward. The enemy soldiers had left the rifle-pit.

Searing wanted to be sure that all the Confederate pickets had gone. He kept his head low, and ran from one rifle-pit to the next. They were all empty. The Confederates had left this picket line. But where were they now?

Searing walked through the forest until he came to the edge of a plantation. Beyond the plantation, there was an old farmhouse on a small hill. The windows of the building were broken and there was no door.

"This will be a good place to hide and watch," he thought.

He went into the building and looked out of one of the broken windows.

Searing stared across the flat, empty ground that was between the farmhouse and Kennesaw Mountain. There were no trees between the farmhouse and the mountain. Half a mile away, he could see a road. It was crowded with soldiers who wore gray uniforms. This was the rear guard of the Confederate regiment. The metal barrels of their rifles shone in the morning sunlight. The Confederates were moving south.

Searing had to return quickly to his own regiment. He had to report to his commanding officers. But the gray line of

The road was crowded with soldiers who wore gray uniforms.

One of the Missing

Confederate soldiers was in front of him. Private Searing had a powerful Springfield rifle. He wanted to shoot one of the enemy. He lifted his rifle and aimed it at a Confederate soldier. But Searing did not kill anyone that bright summer morning. And he did not make a report about the enemy's movements.

On the side of Kennesaw Mountain, a Confederate captain was standing beside a cannon. The distance between the cannon and the farmhouse was two miles. The captain saw the group of Yankee officers on the hill to the north. He aimed the cannon at them, and fired. But the shell missed the Union soldiers and flew off in a different direction.

Private Searing was aiming his rifle at the Confederates on the road. Suddenly he heard a whistling sound in the air. The sound became louder. Before he could fire the gun, the roof of the house fell in.

When Searing opened his eyes, he saw blue sky. Where was the roof of the house? He was half-sitting and half-lying on the floor, and there were heavy wooden beams all around him. The beams had been the roof of the house. Searing could not move and he was covered in dust. The gray dust covered his body, face, clothes and hair. A large beam was lying across his legs. The scout's left hand was trapped under many heavy pieces of wood. Searing could only move his right arm. In front of his eyes, the scout saw a ring of shining metal. The ring was, in fact, the muzzle of his Springfield rifle. The gun was also trapped among the pieces of wood and other parts of the roof. And it was aimed at the center of Searing's forehead.

One of the Missing

The powerful rifle was loaded with a bullet. It was ready to fire. Searing did not like to look down the muzzle of his own gun. He tried to move his body.

"What is holding my head?" he asked himself. He was able to move one piece of wood a little. Then he stopped.

"The rifle might fire if I move suddenly," he thought. "It looks closer to my head now."

Searing closed his eyes. "I can't get out," he said to himself. "I can't move. I'll sleep now. The Confederates have gone and some of our own soldiers will come here soon. They'll find me."

The scout was extremely tired, but he did not sleep. He felt a pain in his forehead. When he opened his eyes, the pain disappeared. But when he closed his eyes, the pain returned. He heard birds singing.

"Help!" he shouted.

He was surprised by the sound of his own voice. He sounded afraid. No one came to help him.

Private Searing could not sleep and he could not look away from the gun. But, at last, he became unconscious[53].

When he woke up again, Searing knew that his hand was bleeding. He could not see his hand, but he could feel blood pouring from it. Then he saw some small, brown animals running over the wooden beams. They were rats! Rats were climbing near the rifle! But the rifle did not fire.

At last the rats ran away. Searing knew that they would return later. Then they would attack him. They would bite his face, neck and hands. He hoped to be dead before that happened.

Private Jerome Searing was a brave man, but he was tired and in pain[54]. More and more of his blood was pouring from his injured hand. He was very weak and he was terrified. He was suffering, and no one was coming to help him. He tried to lift a small piece of wood with his right hand.

"Can I move the piece of wood so that it touches the rifle?" he thought. "Maybe I can push the rifle so that it isn't aimed at my head."

Searing slowly moved the piece of wood along the barrel of the gun. He could not push the barrel away, but now he could feel the trigger of the rifle. He knew that he wanted to die now. He closed his eyes and pushed the wood against the trigger. Nothing happened. The rifle did not fire.

Private Jerome Searing knew that the pain in his head was part of his dream. He dreamed that the bullet went into his head. At last, the fear of the bullet killed him.

Lieutenant Adrian Searing looked at his watch. The time was eighteen minutes past eight.

The lieutenant was in command of the Yankee pickets on the hill. He knew that his brother, Private Jerome Searing, was scouting somewhere near the hill. Adrian was waiting for Jerome to return and report about the enemy's pickets.

Suddenly, Adrian Searing heard a noise in the distance. It was like the sound of a building falling down. The sound was coming from the south. At the same moment, an officer came toward him.

"Lieutenant Searing," said the officer, "The colonel orders you to move your men forward. You must look for the enemy. We think that the Confederates have retreated."

The lieutenant ordered his men to move down the hill. They went through the forest and came to the edge of the plantation. A wooden farmhouse had stood on a small hill

One of the Missing

beside the plantation. The building was now destroyed. The walls and the roof had fallen. The Yankees passed by on both sides of the house and moved toward Kennesaw Mountain.

Lieutenant Searing came to the farmhouse. He looked inside the building and saw the body of a dead man. The body was buried under a pile of big, wooden beams. It was completely covered with gray dust. The man's uniform was gray. His skin and hair were gray. His pale face was very thin and his eyes were staring in terror. The ground beneath his body was soaked with blood.

"I guess that this Confederate has been dead for a week," the lieutenant said to himself. "Maybe he was killed when the building fell."

Lieutenant Searing did not recognize the face of the dead man and he did not see the Springfield rifle. He looked at his watch. The time was six forty. He followed his soldiers toward Kennesaw Mountain.

THE STRANGER

It was night and we were sitting around a camp fire in the Arizona desert. In this dry, empty land of rocks and high hills, we had seen only snakes and birds. We had seen no other people. Beyond the light of our fire, the darkness was like a black wall.

Suddenly, a stranger walked into our camp and sat down.

"You're not the first men to explore[55] this desert," he said.

We were astonished. Several men in our group put their hands on their guns. But the stranger took no notice of this. He went on speaking and we listened.

"Four men came here thirty years ago," the stranger said. "Their names were Ramon Gallegos, William Shaw, George Kent and Berry Davis. They came from the town of Tucson. They were going to California. Ramon Gallegos, William Shaw, George Kent and Berry Davis were traveling west. They were crossing the desert without a guide."

The stranger repeated the four names. His voice was soft and he spoke slowly. Later, we asked each other these questions. *Where had this man come from? Was he alone? Where was his own camp? Why was he in the middle of this desert?* We guessed that the stranger was a lonely traveler who wanted the company of other men. A man can go crazy if he is alone in this empty place.

The stranger was on the other side of our camp fire. I could not see his face clearly because my hat was pulled down over my forehead. I lifted the brim a little. What did the stranger look like? Well, there was nothing unusual about the

The Stranger

man. He looked like any of our own men. We were all wearing broad hats and he was wearing one too. We looked and listened as he told his story. Later, we remembered his words, but not his face.

"This place was different thirty years ago," the stranger said. "Only Apache Indians[56] and a few soldiers lived here. Many men have disappeared in this desert. The Apaches killed some of them. Others died of thirst because they could not find any water. The Apaches killed strangers slowly, and in a terrible way. We did not want to meet them."

The stranger was silent for a few seconds, then he went on with his story.

"The four of us—Ramon Gallegos, William Shaw, George Kent and Berry Davis—traveled only a few miles each day. Some days we found water, but on other days, we and our horses were thirsty. The heat of the day was terrible, so we traveled at night. Why were we crossing the desert? We were going to California, to find gold.

"We had come many miles," the stranger went on. "We couldn't turn back. After many days, we came to some mountains where we found a little water, and some wild animals. We were able to shoot several of the animals, so at last we had some food. We ate and slept, and soon we felt stronger. But a few days later, the Apaches found us."

The stranger stared at the flames of the fire as he spoke.

"The Indians were behind us," he said. "They started shouting. They had rifles and they started firing them at us. There were about forty Apaches, and only four of us. We could not fight them all. We tried to hide in the mountains but the Apaches followed us closely. At last, we came to a steep cliff. We couldn't escape now—we were trapped. What

The Stranger

could we do? We took our guns and left our horses at the bottom of the cliff. Then we started to climb up the wall of rock. There were four of us—Ramon Gallegos, William Shaw, George Kent and Berry Davis."

"We've heard those names before," said one of our own men. "Tell us what happened."

The stranger took no notice of these words. He continued his story.

"We climbed up the steep cliff and found the entrance of a cave," he said. "The Apaches didn't follow us immediately. They were busy with our horses. They looked at the equipment that our horses were carrying. While the Apaches were stealing our equipment, we went into the cave. The entrance of the cave was narrow, and we could shoot anyone who came into it. But we had a problem. We could *not* get out at the back of the cave. For a while, we were safe from the Apaches. But we were not safe from hunger and thirst.

"The Apaches made their camp outside the cave. We saw the light of their camp fire. They were waiting for us to come out. They knew that we would become hungry and thirsty. We would have to leave the cave after two or three days, because we had no food or water. When we came out of the cave, the Apaches would kill us…slowly.

"We stayed in that cave for three days and three nights," said the stranger. "We took turns to sleep. While three slept, one of us guarded the others. But we had no food and no water. No man can live for long in this desert without water. A man goes crazy without water. First he goes crazy, and then he dies.

"Ramon Gallegos died first," said the stranger. "He died in

"While the Apaches were stealing our equipment, we went into the cave."

The Stranger

the morning, on the fourth day. 'I'm going to die today,' Ramon said to us. 'But the Apaches won't kill me.' Then he took out his gun. He put the muzzle to his head and fired. And so Ramon Gallegos escaped from hunger and thirst. And he escaped from the Apaches. That left three of us—William Shaw, George Kent and Berry Davis.

"I was the leader," the stranger said. "I spoke to the others. 'Ramon Gallegos was a brave man,' I told them. 'He knew when to die, and he knew how to die. It's foolish to go crazy from thirst. And none of us wants to be slowly killed by the Apaches. Let's join Ramon Gallegos.' William Shaw and George Kent agreed with these words.

"I laid the body of Ramon Gallegos on the ground and put a handkerchief over his face. Then William Shaw pointed toward Ramon's body. 'I want to be as peaceful as him,' he said. George Kent agreed with him.

"A few minutes later, William Shaw and George Kent put the muzzles of their own guns to their heads. Then they fired. I laid their bodies beside Ramon Gallegos, and covered their faces with their handkerchiefs."

One of the men in our group stood up suddenly. "And you!" he shouted at the stranger. "You let your friends die, and you escaped! We ought to shoot *you!*"

The captain of our group took hold of the man's arm.

"Quiet, now," he said. "You're listening to a story. This stranger has been in the desert a long time."

"The stranger has told us four names," I said. "His story is about four men. Is he the fifth man? How does he know this story? It can't be true."

"It's an old story," said our captain, "And there is some truth in it. I heard the story when I was younger. Many years

The Stranger

ago, the army found the bodies of four men in the desert. The soldiers said that the Apaches had killed the men. The men's bodies were buried near the entrance of a cave. I think that the soldiers found the bodies somewhere near here. This stranger is telling us the same story. But there was never a fifth traveler."

Suddenly the stranger stood up and stepped away from the camp fire. The flames of the fire were low—they gave only a little light. Beyond the firelight, there was darkness.

"There were only four men..." the stranger said, "...Ramon Gallegos, William Shaw, George Kent and Berry Davis." Then he turned and disappeared into the dark, black night.

At that moment, one of our men ran into the camp. He had been guarding our horses.

"There are three men near the camp!" the guard said. "I've been watching them. They're standing out there."

The guard pointed beyond the light of the fire. "The men have been there for a while," he said. "Something strange is happening here! The men don't move, and they don't speak. They're just standing outside our camp. Who *are* they? Are they waiting for something—or someone? They're frightening me."

"Ramon Gallegos, William Shaw and George Kent," I said. "I guess that we've been talking to Berry Davis."

"What kind of fools walk around here at night?" asked the guard. "They're standing in the dark, outside our camp. They don't speak and they don't move. I didn't know if we were in danger. I might have shot them. I might have killed them."

"You can't kill them," said our captain. "They're already dead."

THREE AND ONE ARE ONE

Barr Lassiter was a young man. He lived with his parents and an elder sister near Carthage, in the state of Tennessee.

The Lassiters were simple farmers. Their farm was small and the family was poor. They did not have enough money to own slaves. But although they were poor, the Lassiters were never hungry. They grew enough food for themselves.

When the Civil War began, Barr was twenty-two years old. The war divided many families. Children disagreed with their parents and grandparents. Nieces and nephews disagreed with their uncles and aunts. Sisters, brothers and cousins disagreed with each other. Most people in the northern states believed that slavery was wrong. Many southerners had owned slaves for many years. They did not want the government in the north to tell them what to do. Barr Lassiter supported the Unionists. The rest of his family supported the Confederates.

Barr could not live in the house. And he did not want to fight for the Confederate Army. He wanted to join the Union Army. When he left the farm, Barr's family did not try to stop him. And they did not say goodbye.

Barr joined the Union Army and became a cavalryman[57]. The two armies fought in the northern states and then the southern states. Barr did not return to Carthage for two years. That part of Tennessee had first been controlled by the Union Army. Then it was controlled by the Confederate Army. Now the Unionists were in control again. Many farms and

Three and One Are One

plantations in the south were destroyed. A terrible battle had been fought near Carthage. Many men from both armies had been killed.

Barr spoke to his commanding officer.

"Sir, my home is near here," he said. "I want to see my family. May I visit them?"

"You can have two days' leave[58]," the officer replied.

Barr Lassiter walked across the fields near Carthage, toward his home. It was late in the afternoon when the young man reached his family's farm. The shadows were becoming longer and darker. Before he reached the farmhouse, the sun had set.

"Will my family welcome me?" he asked himself. "I've been away for two years. Have they changed their minds[59] about the war? War changes many things. I've seen and done many terrible things. I'm only twenty-four, but I feel like an old man."

The moon was now shining in the dark sky. Barr walked up to his home. No lights shone from the windows, and the door was wide open. Suddenly, a man came out of the house.

"Father!" the young man called out. "Father!"

The man looked at his son, but said nothing. He turned around and went back into the house.

Barr was very disappointed. He was not welcome in his own home. But he entered the house, and went into the kitchen.

His mother was sitting by the fireplace. No fire was lit and no food was cooking. The fireplace was filled with cold, black ash[60].

"Mother!" the young man called out. "Mother!"

She looked at him, but she did not speak. Barr moved

His mother was sitting by the fireplace. No fire was lit and no food was cooking.

Three and One Are One

closer. He wanted to put his hand on his mother's shoulder.

Then suddenly Barr's sister came into the room. She looked at her brother, but said nothing. She turned around and left. Barr turned back to his mother. But she had left the room too. His family did not want him there.

Barr walked to the front door and looked outside. The moonlight shone on the garden. The long grass moved slowly backward and forward. It looked as if it was moving under water. The wind blew and the trees and their black shadows moved. It was a sad and strange scene. Barr felt tears on his face. He walked back to the army camp.

―――

Barr was tired when he awoke the next day. He had not slept well—he had dreamed strange dreams.

"Did I walk home?" he asked himself. "Or did I dream about my walk to Carthage? Did my family turn away from me? I'm not sure. I must go back to the farm."

He had not walked far, when he met his friend—Bushrod Albro. Barr had known Bushrod for many years. They had attended the same school.

"I'm going home," said the cavalryman. "I'm going to visit my family."

Bushrod looked quickly at Barr, but said nothing. Barr did not notice his friend's silence. He continued talking.

"I know that my family haven't changed their minds," he said. "But—"

"There *have* been changes," Bushrod said. "I'll go with you. We can talk as we go."

Bushrod did not talk on the journey. He was silent until they reached the farm.

Instead of a farmhouse, the two friends found only broken

walls that had been burned by fire. All the doors, windows and furniture had burned. They had become black ash.

Barr stared in astonishment.

"I didn't know how to tell you the truth," said Bushrod. "A year ago, there was a battle here. Your house was hit by Yankee shells. There was a fire."

"And my family—where are they?"

"They're in Heaven, I hope," replied Bushrod. "They were all killed when the house was destroyed."

KILLED AT RESACA

The best soldier in our regiment was Lieutenant Herman Brayle. Brayle's home was in Ohio. None of us knew him well, but our general liked him.

Lieutenant Brayle was a tall and handsome man. He had gray-blue eyes and long blond hair. His shoulders were wide and he had long legs. He always wore his best uniform, even when he was in a battle. He was a well educated gentleman, and he was about thirty years old. Artists like to paint pictures of soldiers who look like Brayle.

Brayle was either very brave, or very foolish. He did not behave like other men.

Soon after Brayle joined our regiment, we fought a big battle. Men were killed on his right, and men were killed on his left. But no weapons injured Brayle himself. He never tried to find a safer position. He walked, or rode his horse slowly, as the bullets and cannon shells flew through the air. Everyone noticed him. The fighting was terrible but Brayle did not care.

During that battle, the general sent a messenger to Brayle. He ordered Brayle to, "Take cover"[61]. This was unusual. The general had many things to think about during a battle. There was no time to worry about the safety of one man. But the general liked Lieutenant Brayle. He saw Brayle's foolish behavior, and he did not want him to die.

In the next battle, Brayle behaved in the same way. He sat on his horse where everyone could see him—including the enemy. Bullets and cannon shells did not touch him. Brayle

Killed at Resaca

stood like a rock in the center of the battle. He did not move, and nothing hurt him.

After that, we decided that Brayle was neither brave nor foolish. He was simply very lucky.

The general also believed that Brayle had good luck, so Brayle became his messenger. Other messengers were killed, but Brayle was never in trouble. He always delivered the general's messages to our front line[62] successfully.

Our front line was often less than one hundred yards away from the enemy. Our men lay flat on the ground as bullets and shells flew over their heads. But Brayle did not lie on the ground, and he did not keep his head low. He simply walked up to the front line, and delivered his messages to the officers there. Then he returned to the general, to give his report.

Other officers in our regiment spoke to him.

"Don't be a fool, Brayle," said one captain. "Take cover. Every enemy soldier is aiming his gun at you. Your head will be shot off."

Brayle smiled. "Thank you for that advice, captain," he said. "If my head *is* shot off, you can say, 'I told you so.' I won't mind."

The captain was killed in the next battle. He was hit by many bullets as he stood in a roadway. Brayle was on the road too. He was going to deliver a message. He got off his horse and pulled the captain's body to the side of the road. The enemy was still firing its guns. Brayle placed the captain's body carefully on the ground. He put the captain's hat over his face. Then he got back on his horse and delivered the message.

After that day, everyone liked Lieutenant Brayle. Brayle was brave and foolish and lucky. We were pleased that he was

Killed at Resaca

in our regiment. When he was with us, we felt safe. We wanted his luck too. But Brayle could not be lucky forever. He was lucky now, but luck does not last.

The regiment reached Resaca, in Georgia. There was only one obstacle[63] between us and the state capital, Atlanta. The enemy had built a line of earthworks[64] at Resaca. The Confederates were behind these earthworks. They were going to stop us reaching Atlanta. The earthworks ran through flat, empty ground and along the top of a ridge[65]. There were trees at each end of the flat ground.

Our regiment stopped moving forward and we camped.

We knew that we were in a good position. Our picket line was in the shape of a half-circle. It went between the two groups of trees. In front of us, there was a big field. The ground was soft and wet and had many stones. It was the kind of rough ground that horses cannot cross easily.

The trees were not a problem. They gave us plenty of cover. But we could not move forward easily across the field. There were too many Confederate guns behind the earthworks. We waited for the Confederates to attack us. We expected them to attack at night.

Our general was in the trees at one end of the half-circle. He wanted to send a message to Colonel Ward, who was at the other end of our picket line. The general spoke to Brayle.

"Lieutenant, take this message to Colonel Ward," he said. "Tell the colonel to move his men forward. They must get closer to the enemy's earthworks. But his men must stay under cover. And they shouldn't fire their guns, unless they can see who is shooting at them. You may leave your horse here."

Maybe the general's order was not clear. Lieutenant Brayle

heard the first part, but he did not listen to the last part. Brayle took no notice of the words, "You may leave your horse here." The general wanted Brayle to walk through the trees and deliver his message. This would take longer, but it was safer.

A straight line is the shortest distance between two places. Brayle went the shortest way. He got onto his horse, rode out of the trees, and across the rough field. He rode in front of the enemy's guns.

"What is that fool doing?" shouted the general. "Stop him!"

A cavalryman rode after Brayle. Ten seconds later, both the cavalryman and his horse were dead. Their bodies were torn open by hundreds of bullets.

Brayle did not stop or turn around. He galloped his horse slowly across the rough ground. Brayle was less than two hundred yards from the enemy's guns. He smiled as he rode through the smoke and bullets. His hat was shot from his head, and his long, blond hair lifted and fell as his horse moved forward. Brayle sat straight in the saddle. He was holding the reins gently in his left hand. His right hand was down at his side. He looked very handsome and brave and foolish. It was like a scene from a dream, not a scene from real life.

Brayle almost reached the trees on the other side of the field. Why had none of the bullets hit him? I do not know. But there was an obstacle that none of us had seen. There was a stream in front of the trees. Brayle's horse could not jump across the stream. The stream was wide, and the water was deep. The horse stopped. And as soon as it stopped, it was shot.

He looked very handsome and brave and foolish.

Brayle and his horse fell to the ground. Brayle stood up. He was all alone and there was no cover. I will always remember that scene. The handsome lieutenant turned toward the enemy's guns and he was hit by many bullets.

Brayle fell to the ground once, twice. Each time, he stood up again. I will always remember the expression on his handsome face. He smiled.

When he fell for the last time, all the Confederates stopped firing their guns. Four men from our regiment walked onto the field. They followed a sergeant who carried a white flag. They picked up Brayle's body.

As our soldiers walked back to our picket lines, several Confederate officers walked toward them. They took off their hats, and helped our men to carry Brayle's body. They carried Brayle back to his own picket lines.

The general gave Brayle's belongings to the other officers in our regiment. He gave me a small book with a leather cover. It was Brayle's notebook.

"Remember Herman Brayle," the general said. "He was foolish but he was very brave."

There was a letter inside the book. It was a love letter. It had been written by a woman called Marian Mendenhall. The address was in San Francisco. The last paragraph said:

Lieutenant Winters has visited me, but I don't want to see him again. He was injured in a battle at Virginia. He said that you were in that battle too. Lieutenant Winters told me that you weren't hurt, because you hid behind a tree. I'll always hate him because he said that. He wants me to think badly of you. I don't believe his words. It's better to hear of a lover's death, than his cowardice[66].

Killed at Resaca

―――

A year later, the war ended and I went to California.

One evening, I visited Miss Mendenhall in San Francisco. I met the young woman in her fine house on Rincon Hill.

Marian Mendenhall was beautiful and charming. Only a brave and handsome officer should be her husband.

"You knew Lieutenant Herman Brayle," I said. "He was killed at Resaca. I was in that battle. This letter was in his belongings. It—it's a private letter. I'm returning it to you."

She took the letter, but did not read it. "You're very kind to bring it to me," she said. "But it isn't important."

Suddenly she looked at the letter and her face became pale. "Uh! There's a stain[67] on it," she said. "Surely, this stain isn't...? It's not blood, is it?"

"Madam," I said, "I'm sorry, but that is the blood of a very brave officer."

It was a cold day. A fire was burning in the fireplace. Marian Mendenhall threw the letter into the flames.

"Uh! I *cannot* look at blood! It makes me ill," she said. "How did Herman Brayle die?"

I stood up. I was shocked. The letter meant nothing to Miss Mendenhall. But it had been written to a brave man, whom I had liked. I could not save the letter from the fire. It was completely destroyed.

Miss Mendenhall repeated her question.

"How did he die?" she asked. She turned her face toward me. The light from the burning letter shone in her eyes. Now her cheeks had become red. The color reminded me of the stain on the letter. She looked very beautiful.

"He was killed by a snake," I replied.

Points for Understanding

OWL CREEK BRIDGE

1 Why is Peyton on the bridge? What is going to happen?
2 Read the description of Peyton's journey home on pages 16 and 17 again. Find three pairs of sentences that show there is something strange about this journey.

BEYOND THE WALL

Dampier says these words to the storyteller: "I believe that a fatal triad has happened to me."
1 What is a fatal triad?
2 Why does Dampier believe this?

AN ADVENTURE AT BROWNVILLE

1 The schoolmaster says to himself: "I did not like this scene". What is he talking about and why did he think this?
2 What does he find out about the man and the two girls from the landlady?
3 What feelings does Eva have for her guardian?
4 "You're a damned killer!" Do you agree or not? Give your reasons.

THE DAMNED THING

What strange or frightening sights did these characters see in this story? (a) Harker (b) Morgan's dog (c) Morgan (d) the coroner and the seven men in the small house.

ONE OF THE MISSING

1 What special work does Private Jerome Searing do?
2 Who does he do this work for and why?
3 Why does Lieutenant Adrian Searing not stop at the farmhouse when he sees his dead brother?

THE STRANGER

1 Why were Ramon Gallegos, William Shaw, George Kent and Berry Davis in the desert?
2 What happened to them?
3 Who is the stranger?

THREE AND ONE ARE ONE

1 Why does Barr Lassiter join the Union Army?
2 When does Barr return to his home? Why?
3 What happens when Barr meets a friend?

KILLED AT RESACA

1 Describe Lieutenant Brayle's behavior when his regiment fights a battle.
2 What do the men in Lieutenant Brayle's regiment think of him? (a) at first (b) later
3 What is your opinion of: (a) Lieutenant Brayle (b) Miriam Mendenhall (c) the storyteller? Give reasons.

Glossary

NOTE: This book is written in American English.
Listen to the audio CD, to help you pronounce the names and places.
The measurements used in this story are *miles*, *yards*, *feet* and *inches*. 1 inch = 25.399 millimeters, 1 foot = 30.479 centimeters, 1 yard = 0.9144 meters, 1 mile = 1.6093 kilometers.

1 **declared independence**—*to declare independence* (page 4)
   independence is freedom from control by another country. When officials make an announcement, they *declare* that something will happen. Or they declare that a thing is true.
2 **supporters** (page 5)
   people who help someone because they believe that person's ideas. They *support* that person.
3 **Fort Sumter** (page 5)
   a *fort* is a strong building that is built by soldiers. A fort might stand by the sea, or a river, or on an important area of land. Fort Sumter stood beside the sea at Charleston, South Carolina.
4 **defend** (page 5)
   fight people or dangerous things and keep them away from your land or property. Someone who fights in this way is a *defender*.
5 **invaders** (page 5)
   large numbers of soldiers who go into a place, or a country, and cause trouble are *invaders*. They are *invading* that place.
6 **commanding officers** (page 5)
   each soldier has a *rank*, or a position, in an army. The chief officer of a group of soldiers is a *commanding officer*. The officer gives *commands* (orders) to the ordinary soldiers.
   Armies are divided into different groups of soldiers. The biggest group is a *regiment*. The commanding officer of a regiment is called a *colonel*. A regiment is divided into groups called *battalions*. Their commanding officers are *lieutenant colonels*. Battalions are divided into *companies*. Each company has two or more *platoons*, and these are commanded by *lieutenants*. The smallest groups of soldiers are called *sections*, or *squads*.
7 **defeated**—*to be defeated* (page 6)
   lose a fight, or an argument. An army that wins a battle *defeats* its enemy.

8 **destroyed**—*to destroy* (page 6)
   break something completely or make sure that something can never be used again. General Sherman burned the farmhouses and the crops that grew in the fields.
9 **surrendered**—*to surrender* (page 6)
   stop fighting and give your weapons to your enemy, because they are stronger than you.
10 **abolished**—*to abolish* (page 6)
    officially stop a law, an agreement, or a way of doing something.
11 **railroads** (page 6)
    metal tracks that trains travel on.
12 **telegraph machines** (page 6)
    machines that were used to send messages. *Signals* (sounds), were sent by electricity, along a cable which ran between two machines. A *telegraph operator* worked in a *telegraph office*. He listened to the messages, or sent replies. The messages were called the *telegrams*.
13 **guarded**—*to guard* (page 11)
    make sure that a thing, or a person, is safe. Soldiers *guard* people, and important places and things, and make sure that they are not attacked or injured. A *rear guard* is a group of soldiers who stay at the back of an army and defends it. See Glossary 4.
14 **floated**—*to float* (page 14)
    stay on the top of the water and move along slowly.
15 **reload** (page 15)
    put bullets into a gun so that it is ready to use again.
16 **cannon** (page 15)
    a large gun that moves on wheels. *Cannon balls* and *shells* are fired from cannons. Cannon balls are large, round, heavy pieces of metal. Shells contain an explosive material. They explode—break into many pieces—when they are fired from a cannon.
17 **recognize** (page 16)
    know a person, or a place, and remember where you have seen them before.
18 **occult philosophy** (page 18)
    philosophy is the study of life. *Philosophers* think about life and how to get knowledge. The *occult* is an old name for magic and mystery. *Occult philosophy* is the study of strange and magical things.
19 **cab** (page 19)
    a kind of taxi that was used in the nineteenth century. A *cab* had two wheels and was pulled by a horse.

20 **old-fashioned** (page 19)
   not modern. If something is *old-fashioned*, it has a style from the past.
21 **improved**—*to improve* (page 20)
   become better.
22 **expression** (page 20)
   the way that your face shows your feelings. Your *expression* shows if you are happy or sad, angry or worried. It shows if you love or hate someone.
23 **not noticed**—*to notice* (page 21)
   the storyteller had not seen the window when he first walked into the room. Now he is looking at the room more carefully, and he *notices* the window. If someone is near you, but you choose not to look at them, you *take no notice* of them.
24 **apartment building** (page 21)
   building that contains many *apartments*—sets of rooms. People who live in apartments pay the owner of the building some money each week, or month. This money is *rent*. The owner of the apartment building is the *landlady*, or the *landlord*. He, or she, *rents out* the apartments to the people who live there.
25 **run-down and neglected** (page 21)
   a building is *run-down and neglected* if no one has taken care of it, or made repairs.
26 **straw hat** (page 22)
   a hat that is made of long pieces of dried grass fixed together.
27 **bowed**—*to bow* (page 22)
   bend your head and the top part of your body toward someone when you meet them. *Bowing* was the polite way that men greeted someone in the nineteenth century.
28 **neighborhood** (page 23)
   people who live near you are *neighbors*. The area around your home is the *neighborhood*.
29 **permission**—*to give permission* (page 23)
   when someone asks you if they can do something, and you agree, you have *given permission*.
30 **Necromantius** (page 24)
   this was not a real person. The name of this character was made from Greek and Latin words for "death" and "finding out the future from the spirits of dead people."
31 **fortune-teller** (page 24)
   a person who knows what will happen in the future.

32 **boarding house** (page 28)
a house where people pay to stay for short visits. The owner of the *boarding house* is a landlord or a landlady.
33 **threaten** (page 29)
make a promise to hurt someone.
34 **suffer** (page 29)
have pain, sadness or terrible troubles.
35 **begging**—*to beg* (page 29)
ask for something in a way that shows you want it very much.
36 **opera** (page 30)
a story told with music and songs. An *opera house* is a large theater where *operas* are performed. The opera, *Rigoletto*, was written by an Italian, Guiseppe Verdi, in 1851. "La donna é mobile" is a famous song from this opera. It means "a woman who keeps making new decisions."
37 **gossiping**—*to gossip* (page 30)
when two people talk about a third person, they are *gossiping* about this person. Their conversation is *gossip*.
38 **guardian** (page 31)
someone who looks after a young person who is not their child.
39 **coffin** (page 32)
a box that holds a dead person's body. The body of a dead person is *buried*—put into a hole in the ground. Then the body is covered with soil. Before the person is buried, a priest says some words in a ceremony called a *funeral*.
40 **inquest** (page 34)
a special court that tries to find the reason for a person's death. A *coroner* is the most important official at an *inquest*. Coroners decide how someone died.
41 **death certificate** (page 34)
a document from a doctor that tells how and when a person died.
42 **undertaker** (page 34)
a funeral director. An *undertaker's* job is to make arrangements for funerals. See Glossary 39.
43 **mill** (page 36)
a place where the power from water or wind drives machinery.
44 **cliff** (page 37)
the steep side of an area of high land.

45 **damned** (page 38)
   something that is evil and comes from hell, is *damned*. If someone says this to you, he or she is wishing bad things to happen to you.
46 **witness** (page 40)
   a person who sees something happen, e.g. a crime or an accident. The person *witnesses* the crime, accident, etc.
47 **swear** (page 40)
   make a promise using strong and serious words.
48 **wild oats** (page 41)
   a kind of grass that grows in wild places. Its leaves and seeds are eaten by birds and animals.
49 **retreating**—*to retreat* (page 47)
   when an army moves back so that it is no longer in danger, it is *retreating*.
50 **picket line** (page 47)
   a line of soldiers who are guarding a place. Each soldier in a *picket line* is called a *picket*.
51 **camp** (page 47)
   a place where people live in special buildings or tents, for a short time. People who are *camping* light *camp fires*, to keep warm and cook their food.
52 **mounds of earth** (page 48)
   piles of soil that have been dug from the ground.
53 **unconscious** (page 51)
   not able to see, feel, hear or think, because you are sick or injured.
54 **in pain** (page 51)
   have a very bad feeling in a part of your body because you are sick or injured.
55 **explore** (page 54)
   go to a place so that you can find out more about it.
56 **Apache Indians** (page 55)
   the Native American people of the southwestern U.S. and northern Mexico.
57 **cavalryman** (page 60)
   a soldier who rides a horse while he fights.
58 **leave** (page 61)
   a soldier's holiday.

59 **changed their minds**—*to change one's mind* (page 61)
   think in a different way about someone or something. If you have an idea and then decide to do something different, you have *changed your mind*.
60 **ash** (page 61)
   soft dust that remains after a fire has burned something completely.
61 **"Take cover"** (page 65)
   the commanding officer is telling Brayle to run to a place where bullets and cannon shells cannot injure him. If a soldier is in a safe place, and his enemy cannot see him, he is *under cover*.
62 **front line** (page 66)
   the area where two armies face each other and fight during a war.
63 **obstacle** (page 67)
   a thing or a problem that you must get past before you can continue on a journey.
64 **earthworks** (page 67)
   walls made from soil that is taken out of long holes in the ground. Soldiers build *earthworks* to keep themselves, or a place, safe from their enemies.
65 **ridge** (page 67)
   a long, narrow top of a hill, or group of mountains. A *ridge* is also a long, narrow, raised line that is along the surface of something.
66 **cowardice** (page 70)
   if you are not brave, and you cannot do what you should do, you are a *coward*. Your behavior is *cowardice*.
67 **stain** (page 71)
   a mark that is left accidentally on something. Lieutenant Brayle's blood has left a *stain* on Miss Mendenhall's letter.

Dictionary extracts adapted from the Macmillan English Dictionary © Bloomsbury Publishing PLC 2002 and © A & C Black Publishers Ltd 2005

Exercises

Vocabulary: meanings of words from the story

Put the words and phrases in the box next to the correct meanings.

> obstacle   uniform   barrel   destroy   rifle   shotgun
> trigger   muzzle   cavalry   saddle   stain   reins   coroner
> pickets   earthworks   scout   inquest   cord   hang
> defend   fort   cannon   invade   undertaker   defeat

1		a strong building, often with a high wall around it, used by soldiers
2		a large and powerful gun, used in the past to shoot metal balls and explosive shells
3		a person sent out by an army to get information about the position and movement of the enemy
4		a long gun that you hold against your shoulder to shoot
5		the part of a gun that you move with your finger to make the gun fire
6		the part of a gun that a bullet is fired through
7		the end of a gun where the bullet comes out
8		the part of an army which has soldiers who ride on horses
9		a leather seat that you put on a horse's back when you want to ride
10		[usually plural] a narrow piece of leather fastened to a horse's head which a rider uses to control a horse
11		sentries – soldiers who guard a place, especially an army camp; in modern American English it means people who protest outside a building

12		a wall and ditch which soldiers dug from the ground to defend a place
13		a long gun that is used especially for hunting birds and small animals
14		strong, thin rope
15		a set of clothes that you wear to show that you are part of an organization or school
16		to kill someone by putting a rope round their neck and making them fall
17		to protect someone or something from attack
18		to damage something so badly that it either does not exist or cannot be used
19		an official inquiry into the cause of someone's death
20		someone whose job is to decide, officially, how someone died
21		an object that blocks the way forward or a problem that stops something happening
22		a mark that is left on something accidentally – often made by dirt or blood
23		to take or send an army into another country
24		someone whose job it is to make arrangements for funerals
25		failure to win a war or game

Writing: rewrite sentences

Rewrite the sentences replacing the underlined words with the words in the box. Use each word only once. There are some extra words.

> camped   reload   fort   upset   be silent   scream   scout
> pickets   desert   gold   cord   obstacle   belongings
> inquest   stain   witness   muzzle   gossiping

> **Example:** His hands were tied with a <u>thin piece of rope</u>.
> You write: His hands were tied with a *cord*.

1. It took half a minute to <u>put a new bullet in</u> their rifles.
   It took

2. Yankee soldiers built a <u>strong place</u> near the bridge.
   Yankee soldiers

3. The people of Brownsville enjoyed <u>talking about other people in the town</u>.
   The people

4. She has had a terrible shock and is <u>feeling sad and angry</u>.
   She has had

5. A coroner held <u>a special court</u> to decide how the girl died.
   A coroner

6. I ask you to <u>say nothing</u>.
   I ask

7. It was the <u>loud cry of pain</u> of a wild animal.
   It was

8. Private Jerome Searing was a <u>man who watched the movements of enemy soldiers</u>.
   Private Jerome Searing

9. <u>Sentries</u> guarded the edge of our camp.

10 What was he doing in the middle of this <u>empty place</u>?
    What was _____

11 We were going to California to find <u>precious metal</u>.
    We were going to _____

12 There was only one <u>problem</u> that prevented us from reaching Atlanta.
    There was _____

13 Our regiment <u>stopped and put up tents</u> for the night.
    Our regiment _____

14 The general gave Brayle's <u>personal things</u> to another officer in our regiment.
    The general _____

15 There was a red <u>mark</u> on the letter.
    _____

Vocabulary: anagrams

The letters of each word are mixed up. Write the words correctly. The first one is an example.

Example:	
ANTIS *stain*	a mark left accidentally on clothes or surfaces

1	GIRED	the long, narrow top of a hill or mountain/a group of hills or mountains
2	RAWCOD	someone who is not brave enough to fight or do something difficult or dangerous
3	ANVARYCALM	a soldier who rides on a horse
4	POLEREX	to travel around an area in order to learn about it or to find something valuable such as oil
5	REARETT	to move back from a difficult or dangerous situation
6	SWINEST	someone who sees a crime, accident or other event happen
7	THADE CATERTIFICE	a paper from a doctor that tells how a person died
8	UNGRADIA	someone who is legally responsible for a child whose parents are dead
9	PIGSOS	conversation about unimportant things, especially about other people's lives
10	TREANTHE	to say you will hurt someone if they do not do what you want
11	GINDRABO SHOUE	a house in which people pay to live as guests with the family who owns it

12	SINOPERSIM	the right to do something that is given to you by a person in authority
13	NOSERPESIX	a look on someone's face that shows their thoughts or feelings
14	LOCCUT	related to magic and secret knowledge
15	GOZENRICE	to know who a person is, or what the thing that you are seeing/hearing is
16	OLIHSFO	to do something silly or without sense
17	DIALORAR	the metal track that trains travel on
18	CREALED	to say officially that something is true or happening; to make an official statement
19	NEDFED	to protect someone or something from attack
20	SORTDYE	to damage something so badly that either it cannot return to its normal state or it no longer exists

Grammar: syntax

Put the words into the correct order to make sentences.

> **Example:** His end on one plank were of a feet.
> You write: *His feet were on one end of a plank.*

1 You have to ring the door or don't knock on the bell.

_____

2 There was a hill on the forest that ran through the path.

_____

3 an Eight small empty of men were sitting in a house room together.

_____

4 The wood of the roof was among the pieces of gun and other parts also trapped.

_____

5 Adrian was waiting about for the report to return Jerome and enemy's pickets.

_____

6 A place can go empty alone if he is in this crazy man.

_____

7 Most wrong states believed that slavery was in the northern people.

_____

8 Our enemy front line was often one less than the hundred away from yards.

_____

Vocabulary Choice: words which are related in meaning

Which word is most closely related? Look at the example and circle the word that is closest in meaning to the word in bold.

Example:
divide   join   (separate)   attach   connect

1	**crops**	police	barbers	cooking	plants
2	**equipment**	food	bags	tools	horses
3	**wealth**	safety	marks	hygiene	riches
4	**mystery**	explanation	weather	unknown	imagination
5	**disappear**	return	attend	travel	vanish
6	**creek**	noise	wood	stream	driver
7	**dawn**	sunrise	animal	view	dark
8	**aim**	shell	point	fire	shoot
9	**guest**	choose	pick	visitor	spirit
10	**silent**	night	tower	light	quiet

Vocabulary: opposite meanings

Look at the example and circle the word which is nearest to the opposite meaning of the word in bold.

Example:
leave   go   exit   quit   (stay)

1	**bright**	light	dim	clear	shine
2	**warm**	hot	red	sunny	cool
3	**strange**	unknown	mysterious	familiar	alien
4	**reply**	answer	request	ask	beg
5	**thin**	long	thick	round	thought
6	**permit**	refuse	allow	approve	agree
7	**soft**	strong	hard	comfortable	smooth
8	**slim**	fat	thin	narrow	small

Macmillan Education
The Macmillan Building
4 Crinan Street
London N1 9XW
A division of Macmillan Publishers Limited
Companies and representatives throughout the world

ISBN 978–0–230–03517–1
ISBN 978–1–4050–8741–4 (with CD edition)

This version of this collection of short stories by Ambrose Bierce
(*An Occurence at Owl Creek Bridge*, *Beyond the Wall*, *An Adventure at Brownville*, *The Damned Thing*, *One of the Missing*, *The Stranger*, *Three and One Are One* and *Killed at Resaca*) was retold by Stephen Colbourn for Macmillan Readers
First published 2007
Text © Macmillan Publishers Limited 2007
Design and illustration © Macmillan Publishers Limited 2007
This version first published 2007

All rights reserved; no part of this publication may be
reproduced, stored in a retrieval system, transmitted in any
form, or by any means, electronic, mechanical, photocopying,
recording, or otherwise, without the prior written permission of
the publishers.

Illustrated by Martin Sanders and Laszlo Veres
Cover by Stone/Getty Images

Printed in and bound in Thailand

with CD edition

2016 2015 2014
10 9 8 7

without CD edition

2016 2015 2014
7 6 5 4 3